# CONTENTS

# FOREWORD

In recent years, Canada's military has participated in important operations abroad, but most Canadians experience conflict only through news reports. Few of us have experienced "total war" in which an entire population was engaged in the war effort.

Some things do not change over generations: the anxiety and apprehension of those whose loved ones have gone off to fight, or the grief felt for those who are killed or injured. Online videos of ramp ceremonies and Highway of Heroes processions rise from the same emotions felt by those Canadians who honoured their dead through scrapbooks and mementoes decades ago. Today's Memorial Cross recipients know the pain of some 100,000 others whose sons, daughters or husbands were killed in the "total wars" of 1914–18 and 1939–45.

In a much more tangible way than today, the First and Second World Wars brought the conflict into the personal lives of all Canadians. By focusing on the real experiences of individuals, the exhibition **World War Women** reminds us of the many ways total war affected all women, both civilian and military, at work and at home.

Canadian women responded to war. Many left their domestic routines to replace men in factories and on farms. During the First World War, women served as military nurses and then took on many non-combat military roles in the Second World War. Women also participated in the war effort by knitting socks and sending care packages to overseas combatants, by conserving scarce domestic commodities and by following the lengthy list of wartime rules and regulations.

Not everyone was comfortable with the shifting gender roles that were part of Canada's social transformation during the world wars. The exhibition shows the challenges women faced when they moved into traditionally male-dominated areas such as factories or the military.

Through the exhibition and this catalogue, we see many facets of the dynamic tension of a society where total war introduced women to new responsibilities and achievements and laid the foundations for some of the most profound changes in Canadian society.

**Stephen Quick**

Director General
Canadian War Museum

# INTRODUCTION

Women contributed to every aspect of Canada's participation in the First and Second World Wars.

These were total wars, meaning that entire populations were in on the fight, whether on the home front or in uniform. Each woman had her own personal reasons for participating.

Canadian women served in the military. They took on paid war work. They volunteered their time, money and energy to a vast array of patriotic causes. They changed their domestic habits to meet wartime demands. And they did it all while waiting and worrying for loved ones in uniform, some of whom they would never see again.

Souvenir of Fire

Parliament Buildings, Ottawa,
February 3rd. 1916.

———

Made from wood of Sir Wilfrid Laurier's door and copper from roof.

Sold by the Ottawa Women's Canadian Club
for the Benefit of the Prisoners of War Fund.

# VOLUNTEERING

Canadian women poured a vast amount of energy into volunteer activities that supported the war effort.

Not everyone was suited to military service or even paid war work, but most women could engage in meaningful volunteer work, often in their own homes and communities. Whether they were assembling care packages, raising funds for war purposes or knitting socks and other comforts for soldiers, women on the Canadian home front turned their time and energy into practical and patriotic contributions.

Women's groups were especially active in volunteer war work. They raised money for the war effort in traditional ways, such as teas and concerts, and through other, more inventive methods. When a fire destroyed the Centre Block on Parliament Hill in 1916, the Ottawa Women's Canadian Club sold souvenirs made from the debris to benefit prisoners of war. This example features a piece of copper from the building's roof and a block of wood from Sir Wilfrid Laurier's office door.

## PROVIDING COMFORTS

Comforts were items that made the lives of soldiers, sailors and airmen more enjoyable. Women sent cigarettes, sweets, canned delicacies, reading material, soap, towels and knitted apparel to military personnel. The packaging and distribution of parcels filled with these small luxuries brought a traditional maternal role into the rough sphere of war.

## SENDING SUPPLIES

Red Cross volunteers fill bags with supplies in Newfoundland during the Second World War.

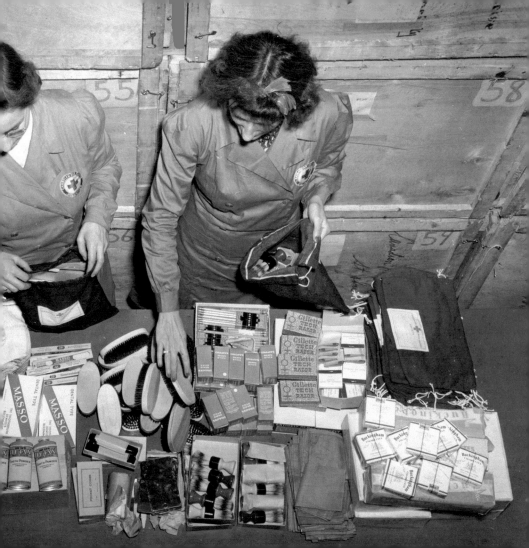

TOBIN'S "PEERLESS"
SOLDIERS' COMFORT BOXES
FOR OVERSEAS MAILING

TO THE SENDER FILL ME TO THE BRIM WITH GOOD THINGS (NOT EXCEEDING POSTAL
REGULATION WEIGHTS) - WRAP ME IN STOUT BROWN PAPER - TIE
ME WITH STRONG CORD - ADDRESS ME VERY FULLY AND
DISTINCTLY - THEN SEND ME ON MY MESSAGE OF LOVE I'LL DELIVER THE GOODS

POSTAL REGULATIONS
TO FRANCE - FROM 1 TO 3 LBS., 24c.  FROM 3 TO 7 LBS. 32c. a LIMIT 7 LBS.
TO ENGLAND - 12c PER LB. - LIMIT 11 LBS.

SOLD ONLY BY LEADING DRUGGISTS, GROCERS AND NEWS DEALERS THROUGHOUT CANADA

J. TOBIN & SONS  IMPORTERS AND  OTTAWA, CANADA
MANUFACTURERS
PRODUCERS OF HIGH GRADE SPECIALTIES

## COMFORT BOX

Sending comfort parcels overseas was a regular feature of life for many women on the Canadian home front. This box, with instructions and postal regulations printed on the bottom, was manufactured expressly for that purpose.

## COMFORT BAG

The Women's Auxiliary of the Navy League of Canada, Southern Alberta Division, donated this comfort bag to the Royal Canadian Naval Volunteer Reserve. The donor's name and address could be included on the bag, so that the sailor who received it could extend his thanks.

**Comfort Bag**
1939–1945

Jas. Prescott & Son, Ltd. London

NATIONAL SERVICE COMMITTEE
REPRESENTING THE WOMEN OF CANADA

CHRISTMAS GREETING
TO OUR BRAVE SOLDIERS
FROM THEIR CANADIAN HOMES.

## WRITING CASE

Women's groups sent practical
gifts overseas, such as this sturdy
waterproof writing case, which bears
Christmas greetings to "our brave
soldiers from their Canadian homes."
Messages such as this reminded
troops that they had not been
forgotten by people back home.

## MARY ROBERTSON GORDON –
## MEMBER OF THE CANADIAN FIELD COMFORTS COMMISSION

Anxious to do her bit, Mary Robertson Gordon travelled to England after the First World War had begun. She wore this uniform as a member of the Canadian Field Comforts Commission (CFCC), a female-run organization with a mandate to distribute comforts to men serving in the trenches.

Women on the home front gathered donations of money and goods. These were then sent off to Britain, where the CFCC would sort, pack and send the items to the front. Gordon, whose fiancé and uncle were both serving, knew the difference that small luxuries could make in the lives of soldiers.

Mary Robertson Gordon's Canadian Field Comforts Commission Service Dress Tunic and Skirt

## KNITTING THEIR SUPPORT

During both world wars, knitting was an extremely important activity. An army of home front knitters turned out a vast array of woollen comforts: everything from socks and gloves to amputation covers.

Knitting comforts answered a practical need. During the First World War, trench conditions were such that clean, dry socks were an absolute necessity; and in both wars, the warmth provided by woollen hats, scarves and other cold-weather gear could make a significant difference in the lives of soldiers and sailors.

Knitting also allowed women to stay connected to those who had marched away, while they waited and worried at home. In an era when gender roles were challenged by wartime needs, it was an activity that fit the domestic role women were traditionally seen to play.

## KNITTERS WITH THE IMPERIAL ORDER DAUGHTERS OF THE EMPIRE

The Imperial Order Daughters of the Empire (IODE) was heavily involved in volunteer efforts during both world wars. Here, Manitoba members of the IODE knit comforts. The woman in the centre is using a knitting machine.

**Mrs. John J. Morrison's Knitting Machine**

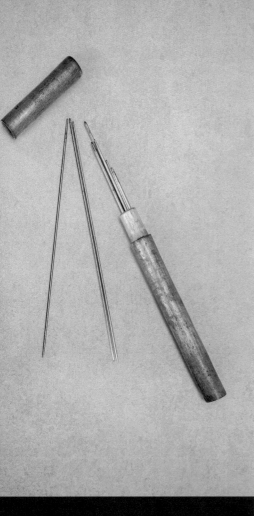

## MRS. MORRISON'S KNITTING MACHINE

Mrs. John J. Morrison knitted socks for the Canadian Red Cross with this knitting machine. These machines helped women knit faster, allowing them to produce the enormous number of socks needed by soldiers serving in the muddy trenches of France and Belgium.

## DAISY MAGUIRE'S KNITTING NEEDLES

Most women used knitting needles to produce the millions of knitted goods needed for the war effort. For an older woman such as Daisy Maguire, the owner of these needles, knitting would have been an excellent way for her to contribute to the war effort.

## MARY ZINIUK'S AIR FORCE YARN

During the Second World War, Mary Ziniuk knitted comforts for her three brothers, all serving in the Royal Canadian Air Force; this ball of yarn was left over from her efforts.

To ensure that the woollen comforts conformed to military standards, knitters used specially dyed yarns that matched each service branch's particular uniform. This ball would have provided enough yarn for one pair of socks.

**4 PLY**

**MILITARY SERVICE YARNS**

## FUNDRAISING

During both world wars, women raised funds through a variety of groups, such as the Red Cross, the Navy League and the Prisoners of War Fund. They also donated their own money, helping to pay for the wars by investing in Victory Loans and War Savings stamps and certificates.

While most of the War Savings stamps were sold in post offices, banks and stores, during the Second World War the government also used young women, known as Miss Canadas, to sell the 25-cent stamps door to door and on street corners.

## CANVASSING FOR THE WAR

Barbara McNutt Eagles poses in the Miss Canada uniform she wore while selling War Savings stamps. She received the pin on her apron for participation and good attendance in the program.

Barbara McNutt Eagles' Miss Canada Apron

## BARBARA McNUTT EAGLES –
## A YOUNG MISS CANADA

Most Miss Canadas were teenagers, but Barbara McNutt Eagles was only 11 when she signed up to canvass in her home town of Dartmouth, Nova Scotia. Her apron, seen here, had to be shortened at both the hem and the shoulders in order to fit.

"I remember that my friend's older sister with her friend covered a route near their home in Dartmouth, Nova Scotia, raising about $5.00 per week, but wanted to move across town to a more affluent area where they could expect to take in $20.00. Although my friend and I were probably under the required age of twelve, we took over the less lucrative route and were issued our uniforms."

— **Barbara McNutt Eagles**, 2007

## ENTERTAINING
## THE TROOPS

Some women channelled their artistic talents into the war effort. More than one million Canadians were in uniform during the Second World War, and keeping them entertained while they trained or waited to go overseas was important to morale. Civilian troupes made up of musicians, dancers and other acts travelled the country, voluntarily donating their time and talent.

## CONNIE LAIDLAW –
## VENTRILOQUIST

Only a teenager when she joined the Hamilton-based Victory Entertainers, Connie Laidlaw brought "Charlotte," the figure you see here, to life, performing 266 shows for servicemen over the course of the Second World War.

*Canadian Women's Army Corps Parade Through the Town*
1944, Molly Lamb Bobak (1922–2014)

# SERVING

Canadian women were limited in how they could serve in the military during the world wars.

Throughout the First World War, prevailing attitudes held that nursing was the only appropriate way for women to serve. Opinions shifted during the Second World War and the military created women's service branches in 1941 and 1942, opening up additional, if limited, opportunities for women. Over 50,000 women served with the Canadian military over the course of the two world wars.

In this Second World War painting by Molly Lamb Bobak, Canada's only official female war artist to be sent overseas during the war, members of the Canadian Women's Army Corps proudly march through the streets. A few members of the Women's Royal Canadian Naval Service look on.

## EDITH ANDERSON MONTURE – AMERICAN EXPEDITIONARY FORCE NURSE

Monture was born and raised on the Six Nations of the Grand River Territory in Ontario. As a First Nations woman, she was prevented by *Indian Act* restrictions of the time from obtaining nursing training in Canada. Determined, Monture attended nursing school in the United States. When the US entered the war in 1917, she enlisted and served at an American base hospital in France.

## HEIRLOOMS OF WAR SERVICE

Monture acquired this trench art — vases made from disused shell casings — while she was in France. The initials "AEF" refer to the American Expeditionary Force with which she served. Monture cherished these items from her time as a military nurse and handed them down to her family.

**Edith Anderson Monture's Trench Art**

1917–1919

**Lieutenant Margaret Mowat's Commemorative Plate, No. 14 Canadian General Hospital**
1944

## MARGARET MOWAT – NURSES UNDER ATTACK

Nursing in active theatres of war could be hazardous. On November 6, 1943, German aircraft attacked the SS *Santa Elena*, a troopship carrying 99 Canadian nurses from the No.14 Canadian General Hospital through the Mediterranean to Italy. The nurses went to their emergency stations when an aerial torpedo tore through the ship's stern and boarded lifeboats as the ship listed. After several hours at sea, they made a difficult 20-metre climb up the side of the SS *Monterey*, which had come to their rescue. All of the nurses survived, although four members of the *Santa Elena*'s crew were killed.

This commemorative plate tells the wartime story of the No. 14 Canadian General Hospital, including the sinking of the *Santa Elena*. This copy belonged to Margaret Mowat, a Canadian nurse who was on board during the attack.

## MARY WEAVER – MEMBER OF THE WENTWORTH WOMEN'S AUXILIARY CORPS

When the Second World War erupted, many women were keen to play an active role. Barred from military service except as nurses, and inspired by British organizations such as the Auxiliary Territorial Service, women across Canada organized their own paramilitary groups.

They wore uniforms, learned drills and other military skills, and adopted rank systems. Lobbying by paramilitary leaders helped pressure the Canadian government into creating women's branches of the regular armed forces in 1941 and 1942.

The chevron on the sleeve of this homemade uniform indicates that its owner, Mary Weaver, served one year with the Hamilton-based Wentworth Women's Auxiliary Corps.

**Mary Weaver's Wentworth Women's Auxiliary Corps Uniform**
1939–1945

## WOMEN'S SERVICE BRANCHES

Beginning in 1941, Canadian women could formally join the armed forces. A looming shortage of military manpower, coupled with a clear desire on the part of many women to serve in uniform, led to the creation of women's service branches: the Royal Canadian Air Force Women's Division, the Canadian Women's Army Corps and the Women's Royal Canadian Naval Service. This photo shows a Canadian Women's Army Corps recruiting parade in Shawinigan, Quebec.

*Private Roy, Canadian Women's Army Corps*
1946, Molly Lamb Bobak (1922–2014)

## EVA MAY ROY – CANTEEN WORKER

While the opportunity for women
to perform military service was new,
much of the work they performed was
not. Initially, they were limited to the
trades society considered acceptable
for women at the time, including food
service, cleaning and clerical work.
By taking on these essential, yet non-
combat roles, women freed up men to
fight. Women took on a greater variety
of work as the war progressed.

In this painting, Private Eva May Roy is
pictured working in a Halifax canteen
— a type of military restaurant for
service personnel.

## LORNA STANGER – PHOTOGRAPHER

Bored with her civil service job, Lorna Stanger applied to all three service branches and joined the first one to accept her: the Women's Royal Canadian Naval Service. Trained as a photographer, she served with Naval Information in Ottawa, Halifax and London, England. This is one of her naval uniforms.

"I also became much more independent — I used to be quite shy and lacking in self-confidence . . . I really enjoyed my time in the navy, with all of the travelling and meeting so many nice people. But above all, I'm very proud that I did my part in the war."

— **Lorna (Stanger) Cooney**, 2001

**Lorna Stanger's Women's Royal Canadian Naval Service Uniform**
1943–1945

## WILHELMINA (WILLA) WALKER – COMMANDING OFFICER

Like many women, Willa Walker had a loved one in uniform. Her British husband had been taken prisoner by the Germans early in the war. She wrote letters to him in code and hid escape maps in his Red Cross parcels: a ruse that was discovered — and abetted — by Canadian authorities. Wanting more direct involvement in the war, she joined the newly formed Women's Division of the Royal Canadian Air Force (RCAF-WD) in 1941. Walker was selected for officer training and finished at the top of her class.

One of the few women to attain the rank of Wing Officer, equivalent to a Lieutenant-Colonel, she became the senior staff officer for the RCAF-WDs and, in 1944, was named a Member of the British Empire by King George VI.

**Wilhelmina Walker's Royal Canadian Air Force Women's Division Uniform**
1941–1944

## LILLIAN GRANT – PIPE BAND LEADER

Bands are a traditional part of military culture, but rarely have they been made up entirely of women. In 1942, the Canadian Women's Army Corps (CWAC) formed a pipe band in the hopes of increasing recruitment and morale.

The military gave Lillian Grant the task of recruiting, training and leading the CWAC pipe band. No piping novice, the Victoria, British Columbia native had begun playing at a young age and had formed an all-female pipe band called the Highland Lassies. At age 23, Grant became the only woman in the world to sport the Pipe Major's insignia on the sleeve of her uniform.

The CWAC pipe band spent the war touring extensively through Canada, the United States and Europe. The skirling of their pipes bolstered morale, encouraged enlistment, boosted support for the war effort and entertained weary troops awaiting transport back home.

## PIPE BAND UNIFORM

CWAC pipe band members wanted to wear kilts to reinforce their status as a true military pipe band. The military tailored and issued kilts, such as this one, but the pipers never wore them in an official capacity. Hemmed just above the knee in Highland style, the kilts were deemed unladylike by military officials.

The uniform worn by pipe band members remained broadly similar to that worn by other CWACs. The only real distinguishing feature was their cap, a khaki Balmoral with brown ribbon and pom-pom.

**Canadian Women's Army Corps Service Dress Kilt**
1945

**Canadian Women's Army Corps Pipe Band Leopard Skin**
1943–1945

## A PIPE BAND TRADITION

Animal skins are traditionally worn by pipe band drummers. Musicians Joan Turner and Peggy Hain wore the pipe band's leopard skin when performing on the bass drum. This is a remnant of that skin.

Known as "Suzie," the skin was presented to the pipe band in appreciation of their performance in Lethbridge, Alberta's Fifth Victory Loan campaign. It became the band's mascot.

## JOAN BAMFORD FLETCHER –
## MEMBER OF THE FIRST AID NURSING YEOMANRY

Some women joined organizations that, while uniformed, were not formally part of the military. Service in these groups allowed women like Joan Bamford Fletcher to directly help those who had been affected by war.

Wanting to be close to the action during the Second World War, Fletcher had joined Britain's First Aid Nursing Yeomanry (FANY).

The FANY was an independent women's organization whose members drove vehicles, provided medical care and, in some cases, acted as secret agents.

At the war's end, the FANY sent Fletcher to Indonesia, where thousands of Dutch citizens were trapped in internment camps surrounded by hostile rebel groups. Fletcher's formidable mission was to transport 2,000 internees — mostly women and children — to a safer area 450 kilometres away. Allied troops had not yet arrived, so she negotiated with the defeated Japanese forces for vehicles, an interpreter and armed troops to escort her convoys.

Over the course of a month, Fletcher personally led 20 separate convoys through the mountainous jungle, dealing with monsoons, accidents, rebel sabotage and a kidnapping. The Japanese soldiers under Fletcher's command were impressed by her bravery in the face of peril. Their commander, Captain Keikichi Tachibana, presented her with his samurai sword, which had been in his family for 300 years.

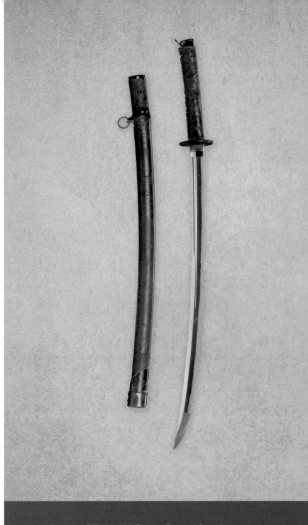

Japanese Officer's 17th Century Samurai Sword, Given to Joan Bamford Fletcher, 1945

MANLY MacDONALD - 18

# WORKING

The world wars created new opportunities for women in the paid workforce, where they played a key role producing the material of war and taking on jobs left vacant by men serving in the military.

The women in this colourful scene are performing vital war work: harvesting fruit to feed soldiers and civilians alike.

## FACTORY WORK

Wearing protective clothing,
the women depicted in this painting
were among the thousands who
manufactured the shells, cartridges
and even aircraft needed to wage war.
Their presence in previously
male-dominated workplaces
sometimes caused friction.

## MARY MAYS' WAR WORKER BADGE

The bar on Mary Mays' badge represents six months' service as a munitions worker. She earned two more bars while making shells for the Imperial Munitions Board during the First World War. The Board was a government agency that directed the production of war material. By 1919, it employed 289,000 workers, 30,000 of whom were women. These badges were specifically designed for women workers.

"My job was to use gauges and test the pieces of work for [18]-pounders. I tended 14 lathes operated by 14 women . . . I received a medal. I have cherished it for 64 years."

— **Mary Mays,** 1980

## ADA SYLVESTER'S HAMMER

Ada Sylvester made aircraft parts with this hammer at the Canadian Car and Foundry plant. Women like her were crucial to the efficient production of the over 2,000 Hawker Hurricanes and Curtiss Helldivers manufactured by the plant during the Second World War.

"You're making the parts for the wings, but there was a lot involved. You had to cut stuff out. You had to rivet things. You had to hammer things in to make it right. I liked doing that."

— **Ada (Sylvester) Dlholucky**, 2007

## NORA GIBSON'S LUNCH BOX – AVOIDING HARASSMENT

Nora Gibson was one of the many hundreds of thousands of Canadian women who joined the wartime workforce. Her lunch box is a symbol of the tension that sometimes occurred as a result of the influx of women into industry. By bringing her lunch to work, she avoided the catcalls and harassment often meted out to female employees who crossed the factory floor to buy lunch in the cafeteria.

*"Boy, did they whistle."*

— **Nora (Gibson) Elrick,** 2007

## MISS WAR WORKER

Public anxieties surrounding shifting gender roles were assuaged by events such as the Miss War Worker beauty contest, which was held in conjunction with the annual Miss Toronto pageant. Pageants reinforced conventional female beauty standards, reassuring society that the women taking over men's jobs had not lost their femininity. Over 100 contestants, drawn from Canada's major war plants, competed for the title of Miss War Worker.

## INGE OSWALD – LENDING A HAND ON FARMS

Food production was a critical part of the war effort. During both world wars, women joined an agricultural workforce that helped feed hungry troops and allies.

During the Second World War, thousands of young, urban women swarmed to the countryside to lend a hand on labour-short farms. Inge Oswald was a teenager living in Toronto when she and her friend Nora Cumberland joined the Ontario Farm Service Force. Sent to pick fruit in Niagara, Oswald's term was marred by a violent allergic reaction to peach fuzz.

## KATHLEEN McGRATH – OCULARIST

Thousands of soldiers returned to Canada with physical disabilities that required care, including damaged eyes. Kathleen McGrath, a trained nurse and laboratory technologist, crafted glass and plastic eyes for ex-servicemen from across Canada. Working out of the Christie Street Veterans' Hospital and Sunnybrook Hospital in Toronto, she began making artificial eyes in 1941.

## NORMA ETTA LEE –
## CONTROL TOWER OPERATOR

In 1942, Norma Etta Lee was hired
by Quebec Airways to work at the
No. 8 Air Observer School as a
Control Tower Operator. The school
was part of the British Commonwealth
Air Training Plan (BCATP). Canada
was a major participant in the BCATP,
training over 130,000 Allied pilots
and aircrew between 1940 and 1945.
Lee was the only female operator at
the L'Ancienne-Lorette airport near
Québec City. She held this position
until 1945, when the school closed.

# DOMESTIC PRESSURE

The state encouraged support for the war effort through propaganda that used simple imagery and direct messages. Women on the home front were subjected to a constant barrage of propaganda, encouraging them to change their behaviour to suit wartime needs.

## FOOD AND EATING

Women were the primary purchasers and preparers of food in most families. Propaganda urged them to think of food as a weapon of war. Canadians were told to follow state rules governing food, to conserve and consume according to available supplies, and to eat a diet that would keep them in optimal wartime health.

This poster, issued by the Health League of Canada, encouraged Canadians to produce their own vegetables at home in Victory Gardens.

## CONSERVATION

With natural resources needed
for the war effort, propaganda
instructed women to conserve
various household products. It
also encouraged them to salvage
materials from around the home, such
as grease, metal pans and rags that
could be recycled for war purposes.

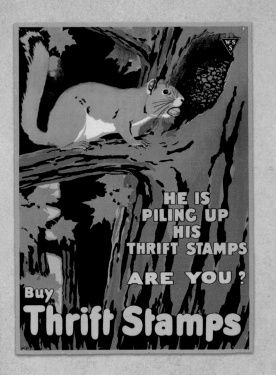

HE IS
PILING UP
HIS
THRIFT STAMPS

ARE YOU ?

Buy
Thrift Stamps

**Thrift Stamp Poster**
1914–1918

## FUNDRAISING

Women were encouraged to support the war effort by buying Victory Bonds and War Savings stamps and certificates. The money they spent would not only help the war effort, but would be of future benefit when the investments paid off after war's end.

## DOMESTIC ECONOMY

Propaganda encouraged women to shop and budget with wartime economy in mind, and to obey all economic regulations. This poster reminded women that under wartime rules, hoarding food was punishable by law.

**Canada Food Board Poster**
1918

## CARELESS TALK

Warnings of saboteurs and enemy agents were an element of life on the home front. Propaganda such as this poster reminded women not to discuss sensitive information, lest it be overheard by the wrong individual.

# WORRY AND LOSS

Anxiety and loss were a major part of women's wartime experience.

Left behind on the home front, women worried about the well-being of friends and family members in uniform, and hoped desperately for their safe return. Most came back, but many did not. Around 115,000 Canadians lost their lives in the two world wars, and many more returned home bearing physical or emotional scars.

## EDNA SCOTT – PUBLIC AND PRIVATE COMMEMORATION

Edna Scott's son Mason was gassed at the front during the First World War. He returned home to Canada, and died of his injuries shortly after the war ended. His family's loss was commemorated both publicly and privately.

The small locket (shown on page 80) was a personal means of commemoration. Inside are photos of Edna and Mason Scott, and Mason's 28th Battalion cap badge is affixed to the front.

After the death of her son, Edna Scott received the Memorial Cross: a public recognition of her private grief. Memorial Crosses were created in 1919, when the government decided to present the mothers and wives of men killed in the war with a distinctive symbol of sacrifice — a silver cross worn over the heart.

Around 100,000 Memorial Crosses — also known as Silver Crosses — were issued for the First and Second World Wars. Each small medal represents a human life lost and the bereavement of those left behind.

SILVER CROSS WOMEN of CANADA

OTTAWA CHAPTER

E R

REMEMBRANCE ASSOCIATION

WE WILL REMEMBER THEM

## SILVER CROSS WOMEN OF CANADA

After the Second World War,
Memorial Cross recipients formed
the Remembrance Association of the
Silver Cross Women of Canada for
mutual support and to assist other
women affected by war. It was also
a way of remembering and honouring
those they had lost.

First used in 1957 during Queen
Elizabeth II's visit to the National
War Memorial in Ottawa, this flag
was the official standard of the
Ottawa Chapter of the Remembrance
Association of the Silver Cross
Women of Canada.

## PERSONAL EFFECTS BOX –
## JEAN CASSELS BOUCHER

For hundreds of thousands of
Canadian mothers like Jean Cassels
Boucher, mail provided a vital link
to their sons overseas. Boucher and
her two sons exchanged hundreds of
letters as the family tried to bridge the
distance war had put between them.

The mail also brought grief. This small
box contained the personal effects
of one of Boucher's sons, Lieutenant
William Robert Boucher, killed in
action on March 26, 1917.

Her other son, Clarence Boucher,
made it safely through the war.

## JOSEPHINE ELLISON GODMAN

On May 10, 1941, during the Battle of Britain, London's Temple Church was set ablaze by German incendiary bombs. A Canadian woman named Josephine Ellison Godman witnessed the destruction, later acquiring this painting depicting the fire.

Godman was no stranger to the devastating human cost of war. In 1917, her husband, Captain Frederick Tyrell Godman, had died in a German prisoner-of-war camp. There was more sorrow to come. In January 1942, her son, Thomas Ellison Godman, was killed in action while serving with the Royal Naval Volunteer Reserve. In 1963, Godman donated this painting, a reminder of her loss, to the Canadian War Museum.

## MINNIE JARVIS

This piece of fine handmade lace
was sent to Minnie Jarvis from
"a soldier friend" serving in France.
The soldier, Lieutenant Evan James
of London, Ontario, had asked Jarvis
to marry him before he went off to
fight. He was killed a month after
Jarvis received the lace.

Jarvis kept the lace in its original
envelope for 62 years before donating
it to the Canadian War Museum.

**Minnie Jarvis's Lace**
1917

"He had asked me to marry him, but he did not want his answer till he came back. He said that if he was badly wounded he would not expect me to marry him, but he did not come back!"

— **Minnie (Jarvis) Smith**, 1979

## NELLIE McCLUNG

These war diaries belonged to Jack McClung, who served in the Canadian Expeditionary Force during the First World War. Upon his return, he gave them to his mother, women's rights activist Nellie McClung, stating that he did not wish to see them again.

Once a pacifist, McClung became a supporter of Canada's war effort after her son enlisted. This shift alienated some of her colleagues in the women's suffrage movement, but her views had been altered by having a son overseas exposed to all the dangers of war. Jack McClung committed suicide in 1944. His mother believed his death was partly a result of his wartime experiences.

"That hurt look in his clear blue eyes tore at my heart strings and I did not know what to do."

— **Nellie McClung**, writing in 1945 about her son Jack's return from the First World War

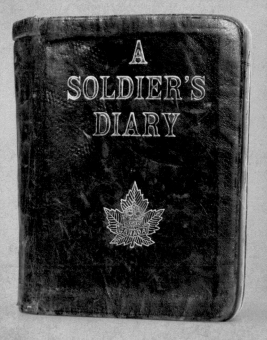

## My Personal Experiences *and* Impressions

OF THE

## Great European WAR

*Which are not for publication unless authorized*

Signed ........................................................

Published by
GEORGE CLARK
128 Bleury Street, Montreal

*Manufactured by*
THE FEDERATED PRESS LIMITED
MONTREAL

Arthur Wilkinson & his

43 Strathcona Ave. Ottawa

Dec. 7 · 1939

mother. Ellie Wilkinson.

## ALTA WILKINSON

Alta Wilkinson's son, Private Arthur Wilkinson, was killed in action on July 18, 1944 in Normandy. She documented her son's war service and commemorated his life through scrapbooks. Their pages include the telegram announcing his death, notes of condolence from the Minister of Defence and King George VI, and a photograph of her son's grave marker.

On November 11, 1975, Wilkinson served as the Silver Cross Mother of Canada. Laying a wreath at the National War Memorial, she represented all women who had lost children in war.

"We listen & read every scrap of news about the Canadians & think of you and pray that God will keep you safe & that it will be over soon. Good night my darling boy. xxxx Mother."

— Letter from Alta Wilkinson to Arthur Wilkinson, returned unread following his death in 1944

## BETTY BUTCHER

The three maple leaves on this service
flag represent Reginald, Joseph and
Lyle, Betty Butcher's two brothers
and fiancé, all of whom served in the
Second World War. Maple leaves
on service flags were overpainted
in a different colour if the person
they symbolized was killed. Both
Joseph and Lyle were killed in the war.
Butcher may not have had the heart
to paint a second leaf gold.

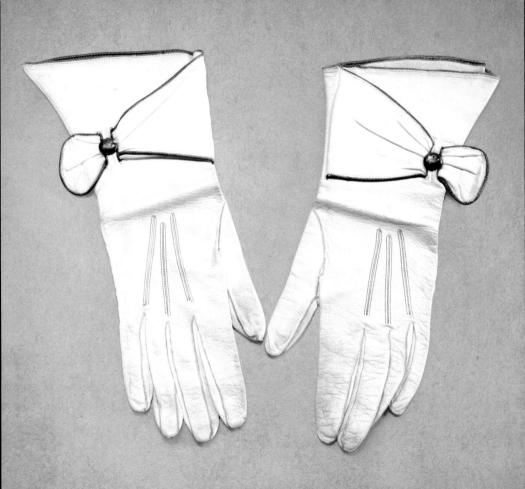

## MARY HALL

On August 24, 1915, Mary Hall wore these gloves as she accepted a Victoria Cross on behalf of her son, Frederick William Hall. The Victoria Cross, the British Empire's highest decoration for bravery, had been awarded to Frederick William Hall after he was killed while trying to rescue a wounded comrade from the battlefield.

The gloves were kept by the family as a reminder of their loss.

# CONTRIBUTIONS

We would like to thank the members of the core exhibition team:
Laura Brown, Krista Cooke, Patricia Grimshaw, Sandra O'Quinn and Bouw Design.
The project also benefitted greatly from the invaluable work of Laura Brandon
and Amber Lloydlangston. We would also like to thank our many colleagues at the
Canadian War Museum and the Canadian Museum of History for providing crucial
assistance and expertise, particularly our colleagues in Collections: Carol Reid,
Maggie Arbour, Susan Ross, Arlene Doucette, Eric Fernberg, Anne Macdonnell,
Meredith MacLean, Lindsay Towle and Kenn Bingley. Thanks also to historians
Andrew Burtch, Nic Clarke, Mélanie Morin-Pelletier, John Maker, Peter MacLeod
and Jeff Noakes. Special thanks are due to photographer Bill Kent and also to
publications coordinator Lee Wyndham for their excellent work in producing this
souvenir catalogue. Finally, we would like to acknowledge the individuals
and institutions whose objects and images allowed us to produce both
the exhibition and this publication.

# PHOTO CREDITS

## Canadian War Museum